CRASHING AND FLASHING

DAVID GLOVER

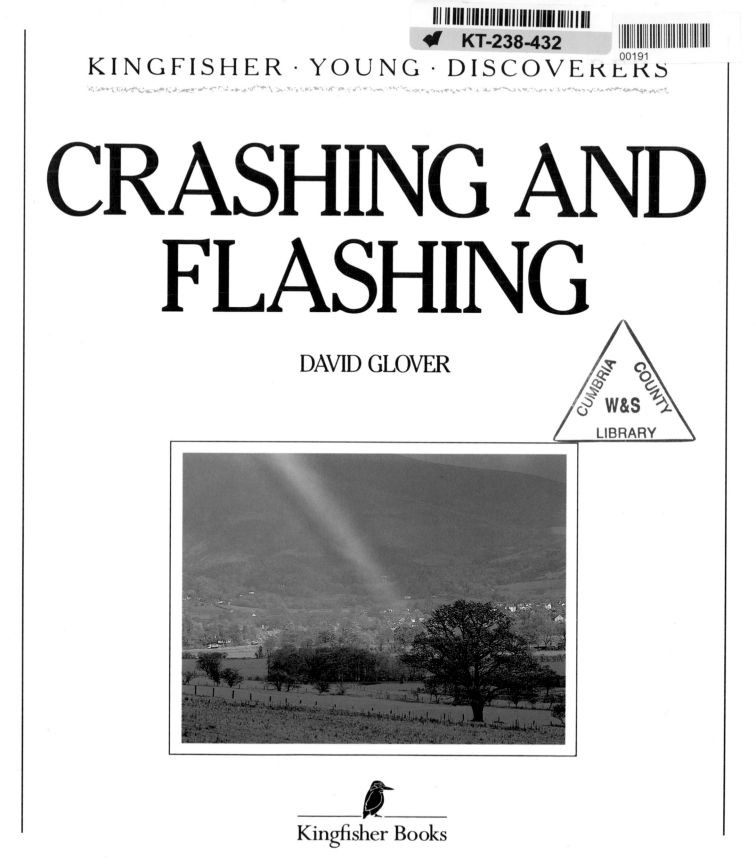

Kingfisher Books

Kingfisher Books, Grisewood & Dempsey Ltd
Elsley House, 24-30 Great Titchfield Street
London W1P 7AD

First published in 1993 by Kingfisher Books

10 9 8 7 6 5 4 3 2 1

BRITISH LIBRARY CATALOGUING-IN-PUBLICATION DATA
A catalogue record for this book is available
from the British Library

ISBN 1 85697 056 6

Series editor: Sue Nicholson
Designer: Ben White
Author: David Glover
Photo research: Elaine Willis
Cover design: Dave West
Cover illustration: Kuo Kang Chen
Illustrators: Kuo Kang Chen pp.2, 9 (bot.
  right), 10 (left), 12 (bot.), 19, 20 (bot.), 21
  (top), 23, 24-25, 26-27 (bot.), 30-31 (bot.);
  David Evans, Kathy Jakeman Illustration
  pp.10 (bot. right), 12 (top), 26 (top); Chris
  Forsey pp.4-5, 6 (bot. left), 8 (top right), 16
  (bot.), 17, 21 (bot.); Hayward Art Group
  pp.16 (top and right), 18 (top right), 27
  (top), 28-29; Hussein Hussein pp.6 (right),
  7, 8 (bot. left), 9 (top); Kevin Maddison
  pp.7 (top right), 11, 13, 14-15, 18 (bot.),
  20 (top), 22, 31 (top)
Photographs: Hutchison Library p.19;
  Kanehara Shuppan Co., Ltd. p.29; Life File
  Photo Library p.24, NHPA pp.17, 29, 30;
  ZEFA pp.5, 10, 13

Typeset in 3B2 by Tracey McNerney
Phototypeset by Southern Positives and
  Negatives (SPAN), Lingfield, Surrey
Printed and bound in Hong Kong

About This Book

This book tells you about sound and light –
what they are and how we use them to hear and
to see. It also suggests lots of experiments and
things to look out for. You should be able to
find nearly everything you need to do the
experiments around the home. You may have to
buy some items, but they are all cheap and easy
to find. Sometimes you will need to ask an adult
to help you, such as when heating up hot
liquids or drilling holes.

Be a Smart Scientist
● Before you begin the experiments, read the
instructions carefully and collect all the things
you need.
● Put on some old clothes or wear an overall.
● When you have finished, clear everything
away, especially sharp things like knives and
scissors, and wash your hands.
● Keep a record of what you do and
the things you find out.

If your results aren't
quite the same as
those in this book
don't worry. See
if you can work
out what has
happened, and
why.

Contents

 Thunder and Lightning 4

 Sound Waves 6

 Feeling Sound 8

 Making Music 10

 Moving Sound 13

 Bouncing Sound 14

 How Do You Hear? 16

Light Waves 18

 Light and Shade 20

 Look in the Mirror 22

 Amazing Mirrors 24

 Bending Light 25

 How Lenses Work 26

 How Do You See? 28

 Light of Many Colours 30

Index 32

Thunder and Lightning

Have you ever been in a thunderstorm? A flash of lightning is followed by a crash of thunder, filling the sky with light and sound.

Lightning strikes are huge sparks of electricity. They are so powerful that they can be seen and heard a long way from a thunderstorm. Light travels incredibly fast. We see the flash in the same second that it is made. But sound travels very slowly. It may be several seconds before the thunderclap arrives at our ears.

The Vikings believed that thunder was the sound of their god, Odin, making his sword ready for war.

Timing a Storm

Light travels a million times faster than sound. So light arrives almost instantly. Sound travels more slowly. It takes about 3 seconds for sound to travel 1 km.

Use a watch to time the number of seconds between seeing a lightning flash and hearing the thunder. If it takes 3 seconds, then the storm is 1 km away. Six seconds means that it is 2 km away, 9 seconds 3 km, and so on.

Eye-Spy

Look out for examples of light arriving before sound. Next time you are at a fireworks display, notice that you can see the rockets explode before you can hear the bangs.

Thunder is caused by the flashes of lightning heating the air around them. This happens so quickly that sounds like explosions are made. The sound of the thunder is carried through the air to our ears.

Many tall buildings have metal rods running down their sides. If lightning hits them, the energy runs down the metal rods to the ground.

5

Sound Waves

If you flick the end of a rope up and down, the 'flick' travels along the rope like a wave – the piece of rope in your hand passes the movement on to the next piece, which passes it on again, and so on. This is how sound travels through the air. When you burst a balloon, the escaping air gives a sudden push to the air around it. This push is passed on through the air like the wave travelling along the rope and we hear the loud bang or pop when the sound wave reaches our ears.

Making a Bang

Bursting an air-filled paper bag forces the air trapped inside the bag through the hole in the paper. This sends out a powerful sound wave through the air that reaches our ears as a loud bang.

Tie a rope to a tree or to a lamp post and flick the free end up and down to see how waves move along the rope.

Passing It On

Set up a row of dominoes, spacing them fairly close together. Now knock the first one over and watch how the wave travels down the line.

6

Do it yourself

Build a sound cannon so you can see a sound wave make a candle flicker. You will need a cardboard tube, some plastic, scissors, sticky tape, a small candle, a saucer and some sand.

1. Stretch the pieces of plastic tightly across each end of the cardboard tube and tape them firmly in place.

2. Make a small hole in the middle of the plastic at one end of the tube.

tape firmly in place or use elastic bands

plastic cut from shopping bag

3. Put some sand in the saucer and stand the candle upright in it. Ask an adult to light the candle for you.

4. Hold the end of the tube with the hole in it about 2 to 3 cm away from the flame.

5. Tap the other end of the tube with your finger. Watch what happens to the flame.

Noisiest Explosion

When the volcanic island of Krakatoa in Indonesia exploded in 1883, the sound wave was heard in Australia, 4000 km away.

How It Works

When you tap the plastic you make a sound wave that travels down the tube and out of the hole at the end. The wave can be strong enough to blow out the candle flame.

candle

saucer filled with sand or soil

Feeling Sound

If you bend the end of a ruler over the edge of a table and then let it go, the ruler will move up and down. When something moves quickly to and fro like this, we say that it is vibrating.

Try moving your ruler so that the vibrating part is quite short. If you can get the short end to vibrate very quickly it will make a sound. This happens because the ruler pushes the air around it to and fro, sending out a stream of sound waves.

Nearly every sound you hear is made by something vibrating.

Feeling Vibrations

When something is making a steady sound it must be vibrating to push the air around it to and fro. If you hold your hand against things making sounds you can usually feel the vibrations. Here are some things to test:
● a purring cat
● a ringing telephone
● your throat when you are singing
● a radio playing loud music

Seeing Vibrations

We cannot see sound waves but sometimes we can see the vibrations that make sounds. Sprinkle a few grains of uncooked rice on some paper, lay it over a radio and watch the rice jump!

turn up sound

press this end down firmly

If you stretch an elastic band between your fingers and twang it, it vibrates and makes a quiet sound. The sound isn't very loud because the band is small and it can only push a small amount of air. To make the sound louder we must amplify it. In other words, we must make the vibrations of the elastic band push more air to and fro.

Do it yourself

Make a sound amplifier. You will need a large plastic mixing bowl, a sheet of plastic cut from a plastic bag, sticky tape, scissors and two elastic bands.

1. Stretch the plastic tightly over the top of the bowl, like the skin of a drum. Secure the plastic with an elastic band and sticky tape.

2. Tape the other elastic band to the middle of the plastic.

3. Now stretch the loose band and twang it.

How It Works

When the band vibrates it makes the stretched plastic vibrate. Because the plastic sheet is much bigger than the elastic band, it pushes a lot more air and amplifies the sound. That's why a road drill makes a very loud noise – it vibrates the ground around it.

9

Making Music

All musical instruments use vibrations to make sounds. Stringed instruments, like guitars, have stretched strings that vibrate when they are plucked or strummed. Wind instruments, like recorders or clarinets, make vibrations when the musician blows down the tube. Percussion instruments, like drums, triangles and cymbals, are usually played by hitting or tapping them to make them vibrate.

Eye-Spy

The next time you hear an orchestra play, see if you can pick out the sounds of the different instruments.

Moving Air

Because a triangle only moves a small amount of air, it makes a quiet sound. The cymbals are bigger and move a lot more air. So they make a loud sound when they are crashed together.

triangle

cymbals

body vibrates, amplifying the sound

sound hole

body

strings

funnel-shape amplifies the sound

The trumpet is a brass instrument. The player makes sounds by vibrating her lips.

Do it yourself

Make your own musical instruments.

1. Make a trumpet with a short piece of hose-pipe and a funnel. When you blow into it, try to vibrate your lips – it takes lots of practice to get a clear note.

2. Try blowing over the top of an empty bottle. If you fill several bottles with different amounts of water, you can get high and low notes. Or you could blow sharply over a pen top to make a high, piercing whistle.

3. Make a rich, deep note with a string bass like the one in the picture. Ask an adult to drill a hole in one end of the pole so you can thread string through it. Knot the string tightly under the top of the box and pluck it. Cut a hole in the box to make the sound louder.

4. Tap small tins, large pans, big empty boxes, or glass jars with pens, spoons or anything else you can find. Some things will make dull sounds which fade quickly. Others vibrate for longer and make bright sounds that ring on.

① tape · blow here · funnel · hose-pipe

Your Own Band

Ask your friends to make musical instruments, too. Then you can start your own band.

③ hole · string · wooden pole · strong cardboard box · sound hole

11

Finding the Right Note

Bass drums and tubas make low notes like the rumble of a large truck or the growl of a bear. Small, light instruments, such as triangles and whistles, produce high notes like the sounds made by mice or small birds.

Violin players can make both high and low notes by pressing the violin's strings with their fingers. When the vibrating part of the string is made shorter, it vibrates more quickly and produces a higher note.

A violin player makes the strings vibrate by scraping them with a bow.

Do it yourself

Make a set of musical pipes with plastic straws, thick card and sticky tape.

1. Ask an adult to soften the ends of the straws in very hot water. Flatten the ends of the straws and cut each of the ends to a point, as shown on the right.

2. Now cut the straws to different lengths and tape them to the card.

cut here

straws

tape

card

blow in this end

How It Works

When you blow through one of the straws, the two pointed flaps vibrate. This makes the air inside the straw vibrate, producing a sound. Air in the shorter straws vibrates faster than the air in the longer straws. So the shorter straws make higher sounds.

Moving Sound

Sound can travel through other things as well as through air. Test this out by asking a friend to tap some metal railings with a stick while you stand farther down the railings. You should be able to hear the sound, but if you put your ear close to the metal the sound will be a lot louder.

Sound also travels well through water. In fact, sound travels five times faster through water than it does through air.

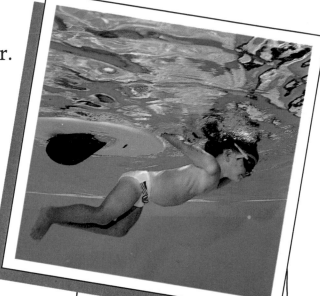

👁 Eye-Spy

Next time you go to the swimming pool, listen to how different everything sounds underwater. (Only try this if you can swim really well!)

Do it yourself

Make a yoghurt pot telephone to hear sounds travel along string.

1. Ask an adult to help you make a small hole in the bottom of each pot.

2. Thread the ends of the string through each hole and knot them. Hold one of the pots to your ear while a friend speaks into the other. Remember to keep the string tightly stretched.

string (about 3 m long)

yoghurt pot

knot

How It Works

Your friend's voice makes the bottom of his or her pot vibrate. This makes the string vibrate, too. The sound waves travel along the string, making the bottom of your pot vibrate and you hear your friend's voice.

Bouncing Sound

If you shout when you are standing in a tunnel or in a large, empty room, the sound made by your voice will hit the walls and bounce back. This reflected sound is called an echo. Echoes are louder when they hit a hard barrier, like the walls of a tunnel. Soft materials, like carpets and curtains, absorb or soak up sound. That's why you will hear an echo in an empty room but will not in one that is full of furniture.

Animal Echoes

Bats find food by making high-pitched squeaks and then listening for the echoes from insects. Dolphins use echoes to find food, too.

Making Echoes

Good places to experiment with echoes are near high cliffs or under bridges.

If you face a cliff and shout loudly, the sound waves will hit the hard rock and bounce back. You may even hear several echoes if the sound is reflected from different parts of the cliff.

Echoes made under bridges are louder than ones made by a cliff because the sounds have no room to spread out.

echo

sound

echo

Do it yourself

Test different materials to find out which ones are better at reflecting sound.

1. Set up the experiment as shown in the picture. Make sure that the cardboard tubes do not touch and that they are about 5 cm from the material to be tested.

2. Move the listening tube to catch the sound.

material to be tested

cardboard tubes

clock or watch that ticks loudly

listen here

move the tube to different angles

paper

cloth

metal

3. Try listening for the reflected sound of the clock's tick against the wall first. Then you could try paper, cloth, a metal tray, a mirror and a cushion. Which materials reflect the sound best? Which absorb it?

How It Works

The strongest reflection comes from hard, smooth materials like metal or glass. The sound bounces off the materials at the same angle that it strikes – like a ball bouncing off a smooth floor.

material to be tested

angle

echo

cardboard tubes

sound

clock

listener

angle

You will hear the loudest sound when the tube is at the right angle to catch the reflection.

15

How Do You Hear?

The drawing below shows what the inside of your ear looks like. The part outside your head catches sounds. Inside, there is a small piece of skin stretched tight like the skin on a drum. This is called the ear drum. When sounds enter your ear, they make the ear drum vibrate. The vibrations are amplified and are picked up by nerves. The nerves then send signals about the sound to your brain and you 'hear'.

hearing aid

Hearing Aids

Some people cannot hear very well because their ears have been damaged. Hearing aids are tiny electrical amplifiers that pick up and amplify sounds as they enter the ear.

How Loud is Loud?

The loudness of a sound is measured in decibels (dB for short). Sounds over 100 dB can damage your ears.

- Aeroplane 100-150 dB
- Road drill 100 dB
- Loud pop music 90-95dB
- Talking 40-60 dB
- Whispering 20 dB
- Falling leaves 10 dB

ear muffs to protect ears

ear drum

nerves to brain

sound enters here

Warning: Never push anything into your ear. If you burst your ear drum you may become deaf.

Do it yourself

Can you tell which direction sounds are coming from?

1. Put on a blindfold and ask a friend to make a sound, sometimes from behind you and sometimes to the right or left.

2. Try pointing in the direction of the sound each time. You could experiment with different sounds (like humming) and distances.

whistle

point at direction sound is coming from

blindfold

3. Try blocking one ear. Does this make it easier or more difficult to tell the direction of the sound?

👁 Eye-Spy

Watch for animals using their ears. Hares can twist their long ears around so they can check where a sound is coming from. Sometimes you can see birds tilting their heads towards sounds, too.

Light Waves

Without light from the Sun, the Earth would be a dark, cold, lifeless place. Light is a kind of energy. We use light to see and to keep warm. Plants use it to grow.

Like sound, light travels in waves. But light does not need to travel through air or water. It can pass through empty space where there is no air or water to carry it. Light waves travel in straight lines, but they travel so fast we can't see them move. We just see a straight, steady beam of light.

cotton

First Light Bulb

The first electric light was invented by Thomas Edison in 1879. He used electricity to heat a piece of burnt cotton so it glowed brightly.

Light All Around

We need light to be able to see. During the day, we get light from the Sun. At night or in a dark room, we use artificial light, such as light from electric light bulbs.

When you read a book by sunlight or by lamplight, the light is reflected from the pages of the book into your eyes. Different things reflect different amounts of light. That is why some things look shiny and bright and others look dull.

Do it yourself

See for yourself how light travels in straight lines. You will need a bright torch and some cardboard.

1. Cut out three pieces of card to the same size and make a small hole in the centre of each of them.

Straight Beams

Sometimes, rays of sunlight are broken up by trees or clouds. You can then see that the light rays are straight.

2. Line up the cards so you can see the light shining through the holes. (You could support them in modelling clay or ask a friend to help.)

3. Now move the middle card from side to side. You will only be able to see the light when the three holes are in a straight line.

look here

Light and Shade

Some things, like glass and water, are transparent. This means that light can pass through them. Other things, like metal and stone, are opaque. They block out the light. As light travels in straight lines it cannot bend around opaque objects, so these things cast shadows. The middle part of a shadow is very dark. It is called the umbra. The lighter edge is called the penumbra.

Blocking the Sun

Light passes through the transparent glass of the window so we can see through it. But the blind is opaque and blocks out the Sun's light.

Do it yourself

See how shadows work.

Put a piece of white paper on a table under a bright lamp. Hold a small piece of thick card or a drinks coaster in front of the light to make a shadow. Try moving the card towards and away from the light to see the how the shadow's shape changes.

Fly's Eye View

If a fly sat in the middle of the umbra, it would see a dark circle blocking out the light. The fly on the penumbra would see part of the light shining past the card.

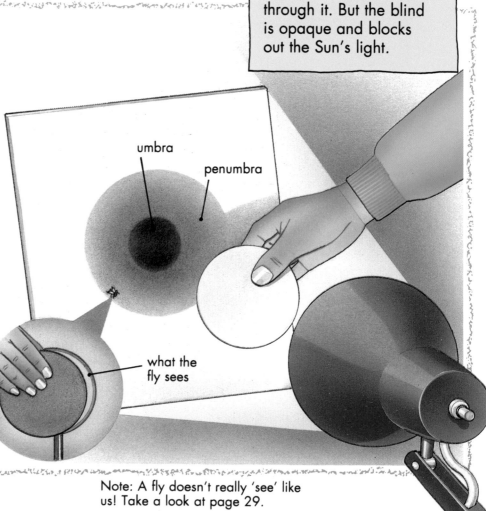

umbra

penumbra

what the fly sees

Note: A fly doesn't really 'see' like us! Take a look at page 29.

Shadows in Space

When the Moon passes between the Sun and the Earth it blocks out the Sun's light and casts a shadow on the Earth. This is called an eclipse of the Sun.

Where the middle of the Moon's shadow (the umbra) falls on Earth there is a total eclipse of the Sun. Where the edge of its shadow falls on Earth there is a partial eclipse of the Sun.

total eclipse– as seen from the umbra

partial eclipse– as seen from the penumbra

Earth

penumbra

umbra

Moon

Sun

path of Moon around Earth

Do it yourself

Your own body is opaque – that's why you have a shadow. Why not set up a shadow screen and play some shadow games.

Use a good, bright light, such as a slide projector. Hang up a white sheet for your screen. Stand close to the sheet to cast a dark, clear shadow.

Things to Try

● Guess an object from its shadow's shape.
● Draw around shadows made by people's faces to make silhouettes.
● Make shadow puppets and put on a play.

slide projector

rope or clothesline

white sheet

21

Look in the Mirror

When light hits a surface, the light rays are reflected, or bounced back. Flat, shiny surfaces reflect light best. That's why mirrors are made of flat, highly polished glass with a shiny silver coating on the back. When you look in a mirror you can see a reflection of yourself. Mirrors can be used to change the direction of light to see into awkward spots – like a dentist looking at your back teeth!

Eye-Spy

If you shine a torch into a mirror you can see how the mirror reflects the beam of light.

Do it yourself

Find one or two small hand mirrors and try these different ways of reflecting light.

1. Can you read the numbers? You could practise mirror writing and send secret messages to your friends.

① ②

place mirror on blue line

2. Catch the Sun's light and send signals.

3. See around corners.

4. Make kaleidoscope patterns. (Place a mirror on each line.)

③ ④

Do it yourself

Make a periscope to look over the heads of a crowd of people or to peep over a wall.

1. Cut out two holes of the same size at the top and bottom of an empty juice or milk carton. One hole must be on each side.

2. Measure and draw two squares on both sides of each hole and divide the squares with diagonal lines. This is to help you make sure that the mirrors are at the same angle of 45°. Ask an adult to help.

3. Cut out two diagonal slits on each side, as shown. They should be just big enough to slide your mirrors through.

4. Slip the mirrors in place with the reflecting sides facing each other.

cardboard carton

mirrors (same size)

cut out

cut out

tape shut

draw lines to get correct position for the slits

45°

45°

mark and cut slits

shiny sides face each other

The picture below shows how the mirrors change the direction of light. Light hits the top mirror and is reflected down to the bottom mirror and then into your eyes.

23

Amazing Mirrors

Many mirrors are flat, but some are curved. A concave mirror curves down in the middle. If you stand close to a concave mirror it magnifies you, so you look bigger. If you stand farther away, your reflection will be upside-down. A convex mirror curves up in the middle. It makes you look smaller but you can see more behind.

Eye-Spy

Look at your reflection in a bright, shiny spoon. In the convex side, you look smaller but you can see a lot of the room behind you. In the concave side, your image will be big if you hold the spoon close but smaller and upside-down if you hold it farther away.

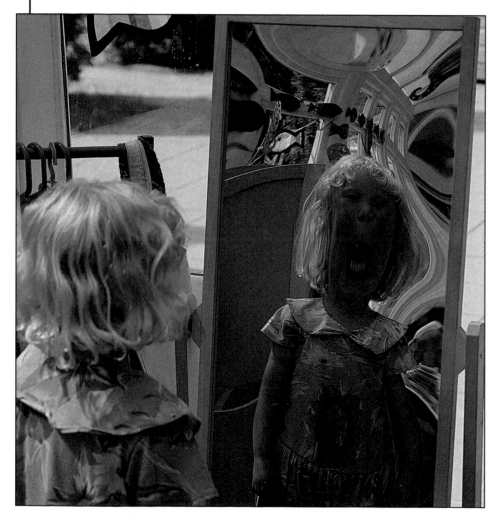

Curved mirrors can be fun! They reflect the light in different directions so your reflection can look stretched, squashed or twisted.

Bending Light

A straight straw in a glass of water looks bent. This is because light travels more slowly through water than it does through air, and when light slows down it can also change direction. This is called refraction. Glass refracts light, too. Look at some stamps through the bottom of a thick glass and see how their shape changes.

Do it yourself

Test refraction with this magic coin trick. You will need a glass, a coin, a marker and some water.

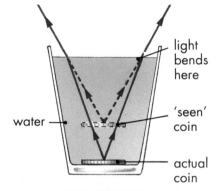

water

light bends here

'seen' coin

actual coin

① look down

empty glass

coin

② look down

water

coin

1. Put a coin in the bottom of an empty glass. Look down into the glass and, at the same time, lower the marker along the side until you think it is at the same height as the coin. Were you right?

2. Now fill the glass with water and try the experiment again. You will probably find that you do not lower your marker far enough. This is because refraction makes the water look shallower than it really is.

How Lenses Work

Lenses are pieces of glass or clear plastic that are specially curved to bend light by refraction. If you look through a concave lens, things look smaller. Convex lenses can make things look bigger. Magnifying glasses and microscopes have convex lenses.

Spectacle lenses help people to see more clearly. We say that people who wear glasses with concave lenses are short-sighted and people who wear glasses with convex lenses are long-sighted.

👁 Eye-Spy

Do you or your friends wear glasses? Are the glasses concave or convex? The box on the next page tells you how to test them.

Do it yourself

Make a simple magnifier to make things look bigger.

1. Cut a hole in a piece of card or use a slide mount.

clear tape

2. Cover the hole with clear plastic tape and use a pencil to drip a single drop of water over it. The rounded droplet should magnify things slightly.

You could also try looking at things through the bottom of a thick glass or a glass filled with water.

Testing Lenses

Collect some old pairs of glasses. First, look at some print in a book. If the words look smaller, the lenses are concave. If they look bigger, the lenses are convex.

Another test for lenses is to look at the shadows they cast on a sheet of paper. Concave lenses spread the light so they cast a big, dark shadow. Convex lenses concentrate the light. Their shadow is small and bright.

convex lenses concentrate light

concave lenses spread light

Do it yourself

Try this experiment with a convex lens from an old pair of reading glasses or a magnifying glass to see how it concentrates light.

Stand opposite a sunny window and move your lens towards a sheet of white paper until you can see an image of the window and the scene outside. The image will be upside-down. The lenses in your eyes work in a similar way. Look at the box at the bottom of the next page.

How Do You See?

Look at your eyes in a mirror. The black spot in the middle is called the pupil. The coloured part around the pupil is the iris. The size of the iris changes to make the pupil bigger or smaller. In very bright light the pupil gets smaller so you are not dazzled. In dim light the pupil gets larger to let more light into your eye. If you go into a dark room after being in strong sunlight you can't see much at first. But after a while your eyes adjust and you can see more clearly.

Looking at Eyes

Close your eyes in front of a mirror and count to 20. Open your eyes. Your pupils will have changed size to let in more light.

How Eyes Work

The lens collects the light that enters your eye and focuses a small picture onto the retina at the back of your eye. (This works in a similar way to the lens you used in the activity on page 27.) The retina sends messages about the picture to your brain. The brain sorts out the image so it looks the right way up, and you can make sense of what you see.

upside-down image

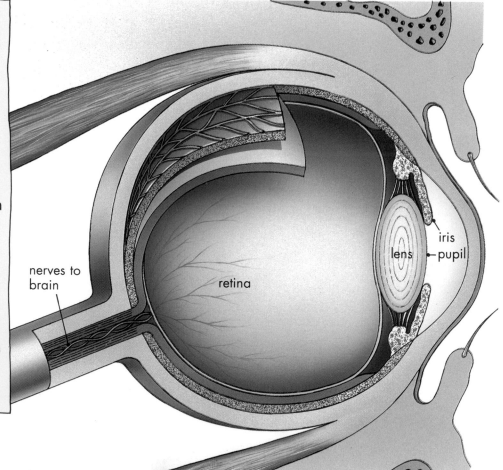

nerves to brain

retina

iris

lens

pupil

Seeing in the Dark

Owls and cats hunt for food at night. Owls have large pupils to collect as much light as possible.

During the day, a cat's pupils are narrow slits, but at night they become wider to let in more light.

day   night

Seeing all Around

A fly has large, dome-shaped eyes. Each eye is made up of thousands of tiny lenses and no two lenses point in the same direction. A fly can therefore see danger coming from most directions – it's almost impossible to sneak up on a fly!

Eye-Spy

Some people are colour blind. This means that they cannot tell the difference between different colours.

For example, someone who cannot tell the difference between red and green may not be able to see the correct numbers in the circles on the right. People with normal sight read the top number as 5 and the bottom one as 8. Those with red-green colour blindness may read the numbers as 2 and 3. A few people are completely colour blind. They see everything in just black, white and grey.

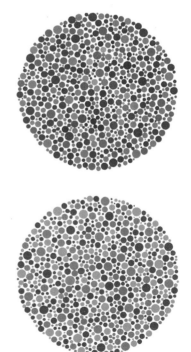

29

Light of Many Colours

Although sunlight looks white, it is really made up of different colours. You can sometimes see these colours when sunlight passes through glass or water. The glass or water bends the colours by different amounts and this makes them spread out in a rainbow pattern which we call the spectrum.

If it rains when the Sun is shining, the raindrops in the air may separate the colours of sunlight and you could see a rainbow in the sky.

Rainbow Colours

A rainbow has all the colours of the spectrum – red, orange, yellow, green, blue, indigo and violet.

Do it yourself

Here are some different ways of making your own rainbows.

Lay a mirror at an angle in a dish of water. Stand the dish in front of a sunny window so that the light travels into the water and is reflected from the mirror onto some card. The water covering the mirror should split the sunlight into the colours of the spectrum.

card

water

mirror

Seeing Colours

Most things do not make light of their own. They reflect light. The colours we see depend on which colours are reflected into our eyes. So a red flower looks red because it reflects more of the red part of the spectrum into our eyes than the other colours.

other colours are absorbed

red light

Look at the world through different colours. Shine a torch through coloured sweet wrappers, look through dyed water (food dye or powder paint works well), or buy coloured light bulbs. These all filter light – a green filter only filters (lets through) green light.

slide projector

CD

slide mount

slit

black card

If you hold a compact disc in front of a slide projector, you can cast lovely rainbow patterns onto white card or a wall. This works best if you put a black slide with a narrow slit in it into the projector. Make one by putting two pieces of black

card into a slide mount. (Ask an adult to help.)

Or you could try just looking at a CD under bright light. The fine grooves in the CD reflect the light, splitting the colours into a spectrum.

Index

amplifier 16

colour blindness 29
colour 30, 31
compact disc 30, 31
concave, lens 26, 27
    mirror 24
convex, lens 26, 27
    mirror 24
decibel 16
drum 10

ears 16
ear drum 16

echo 14-15
eclipse 21
electricity 5
eyes 28-29

glasses 26, 27
guitar 10

hearing aid 16

iris 28

lens 26-27, 28
light, colour of 30, 31
    speed of 4, 25
light waves 18
lightning 4, 5
long-sight 26

magnifying glass 26
mirror 22-23, 24
Moon 21

musical sounds 10, 11, 12

opaque 20

penumbra 20
percussion instruments 10
pipes 12
pupil 28

rainbow 30, 31
reflection, of light 18, 22, 24
    of sound 14-15
refraction 25
retina 28

shadows 20, 21
short-sight 26
sound, speed of 4, 13
sound waves 6-7, 8, 14
spectrum, colour 30
string instruments 10
Sun 18, 19, 20

thunder 4
thunderstorm 4, 5
transparent 20
triangle 10
trumpet 10

umbra 20
underwater sound 13

vibration 8, 9
violin 12